COOL CATS
COLORING BOOK

Noelle Dahlen

DOVER PUBLICATIONS, INC.
Mineola, New York

This cute and cuddly coloring collection features thirty adorable illustrations of cats and kittens—doing ballet, perched in a treetop, playing with yarn, and other whimsical scenes. Detailed designs are perfect for the enthusiastic colorist, plus the perforated pages make displaying finished work easy!

Bibliographical Note

Cool Cats Coloring Book, is a new work,
first published by Dover Publications, Inc. in 2015.

International Standard Book Number

ISBN-13: 978-0-486-80058-5
ISBN-10: 0-486-80058-X

Manufactured in the United States by RR Donnelley
80058X02   2015
www.doverpublications.com

Draw Your Own Cool Cat Design